Keeping a Level Head of Faith in the Midst of a Pandemic

ISIAH BENNETT

Copyright © 2022 Isiah Bennett
All rights reserved
First Edition

Fulton Books
Meadville, PA

Published by Fulton Books 2022

ISBN 978-1-63985-165-2 (paperback)
ISBN 978-1-63985-166-9 (digital)

Printed in the United States of America

CONTENTS

Preface 5
Introduction 11
Prelude Introduction 15

Phase 1: Laying the Foundation 19
Phase 2: Building the Walls upon Our Foundation 32
Phase 3: Installing the Insulation for Our
          Spiritual Walls 41
Phase 4: Attaining Our Permit 50
Phase 5: Adding Light to Our Spiritual Houses 58
Phase 6: Adding the Roof and Trusses on Our
          Spiritual Building 65
Phase 7: The Crowning Moment of Perfection
          and Completion 72

Epilogue 89

PREFACE

The power of God is extraordinary. When I was first given the assignment to write this book, I knew there would be many challenges. God began to give me the divine inspiration to meet these challenges. I am sensitive to his voice. As God began to speak within my spirit, this book started to come together. I know this is the will of the Lord. My inner thoughts were, *Who would want to read this book? I am not a scholar of theology, I completed high school and attended college, but due to family obligations, I did not complete my degree.* However, I have completed classes in Old Testament survey, New Testament survey, Christological preaching, seeing Christ through the Scriptures, hermeneutics, homiletics, basic theology, Hebrew and Greek word study.

As you can see, the route the Lord laid out for me has been different from many other Gospel preachers. I sometimes feel like the early disciples in the Bible who followed Jesus around from town to town, witnessing his mighty works. Jesus told his disciples according to John 14:26 (KJV), "But the Comforter, which is the Holy Ghost, whom the Father will send in my name, he shall teach you all things, and bring all things to your remembrance, whatsoever I have said unto you." Acts 4:13 says, "Now when they saw the boldness of Peter and John and perceived that they were unlearned and ignorant men, they marveled, and they took knowledge of them that they had been with Jesus." So I guess, I would be considered educated in his Word through the Holy Spirit, just like the early disciples.

I have been inspired by many people in my life. I would like to share some of them with you. My wife, Cheryl, of almost thirty years has worked harmoniously with me in the ministry. She understands the sacrifices it takes to be married to someone who has dedicated his life to the purpose of serving the Almighty God. We have five adult children, three live in the city and work in the ministry in some capacity. Our daughter Tori serves as youth director. Our sons Joshua and Josiah serve in the music ministry. I am so thankful for our thirteen grandchildren, and I was exceptionally inspired by my grandson Mason while writing this book. My mom, Stella Osborne Bennett, had gone home to glory (I miss her so much).

She always said to me, "God has a special calling on your life."

My oldest sister, Inell Tina Martin, "the Queen," and my brother-in-law, Deacon Leroy Martin, have always supported and encouraged me. My brother the late Reverend Michael Bennett, who had also gone home to glory, prophesied of my calling many years before I accepted it. My cousin Rev. Dr. Theophile Vaurice and I would spend many hours studying the scriptures when he visited from Ohio. My former assistant pastor the late Dr. James McCarther, who had gone on to his reward in heaven, demonstrated impeccable faith that had inspired me mightily. My pastor and friend the late Reverend Edward D. Lairry of Greater New Hope Baptist Church in North Little Rock, Arkansas, laid my spiritual foundation, which has been so invaluable to me. Others who inspired me include the following: my good friend and brother, former pastor of the St. John Baptist Church in Omaha, Nebraska, Dr. Gregory Ashley who held late-night Bible studies with me whenever he was in town and during our phone conversations; my pastor and friend Dr. Gerald Parker Sr., pastor of the Pilgrim Progress Baptist Church, North Little Rock, Arkansas, who conducted ministry classes on Saturdays that laid my foundation in Hebrew and Greek word study; Dr. D. L. Richardson, pastor of the First Baptist Church, North Little Rock, Arkansas, and the lecturer at the Greater Little Rock Baptist Pastors and Ministers Conference, who hosted teaching, which richly enlarged my understanding of the doctrine in theology; Dr. Rick Rigsby who I met during revivals at Friendly Chapel where my friend Brother Paul Holderfield serves as a pastor; and Dr. Al B. Morgan, pastor of the Emmanuel Baptist Church and my big brother in the Gospel, who has always inspired me with his wisdom, sincere love, and dedication to seek after the righteousness of Christ.

Mother Lynda Gary has become like a mother to me since the passing of my biological mother. She has been so encouraging for me to continue the teaching and preaching of the Gospel of Christ despite this current pandemic. My good friend Dr. R. S. Maxwell, pastor of the Center Ridge Missionary Baptist Church, played a vital role in the quest to remain faithful to God throughout this pandemic. Rev. Dr. Gregory Hughes, pastor of the Pleasant Hill Baptist Church, is my mentor and big brother in the Gospel. My good friend and brother Rev. Robert Thomas, pastor of the Christian Fellowship Baptist Church, Pine Bluff, Arkansas, stood by my side faithfully when I pastored my first church in Tucker, Arkansas. My current pastor, Dr. Luther Green Jr., of Greater New Hope Baptist Church, North Little Rock, Arkansas, with his weekly minister classes helped me obtain a deeper understanding of the scriptures.

Dr. Terry Arvie, pastor of the Mt. Nebo Baptist Church, Omaha, Nebraska, has always opened his doors for me to share the Gospel whenever I was in town. Dr. Thomas Smith, pastor of the Paradise Baptist Church, Omaha, Nebraska, is also one of my fathers in the Gospel when I am away from home, and he graciously shares his pulpit with me. Rev. Harry Nobel, pastor of the New Bethel Missionary Baptist Church, afforded me the opportunities to evangelize in revival. Pastor Robert James thought highly enough of me to be his guest evangelist in revival several times and allowed me to install him in his pastoral assignment at his last church. Finally, I would like to thank my newfound friend and brother Dr. Donald M. Sanders, pastor of the Rock of Calvary Christian Church of Memphis, Tennessee, also for allowing me to minister at his church. I was always told that people do not have to be kind to you. To these people, I give special thanks and deep appreciation for all the love and knowledge they have bestowed upon me.

There are many others who have respected and supported my ministry that hold a special place in my heart, and I believe you know who you are. And I give special thanks to you. Last but certainly not the least, all the officers and members of the Greater New Hope Baptist Church of Little Rock, Arkansas, whom I have been given the great privilege of pastoring over the past fourteen years. Your support and dedication to the vision God has given me is very much appreciated. I am so grateful to serve as your pastor.

To my heavenly Father, Jehovah God; my Lord and Savior, Jesus Christ; and my comforter, guide, and teacher, the Holy Spirit, I give all praise, glory, and honor for your sovereignty. Whom God has sealed unto the day of redemption by the shedding of his Son's precious blood on the cross of Calvary and has signed my name in the Lamb's Book of Life, I thank you for your divine providence for planning my life and all the people who are mentioned and not mentioned. Those who have strategically become a part of your grand scheme in the life that is now and that which is to come. The preface for this book is uniquely by you and to you because he is "the grand Conductor and Orchestrator" and the Author and Finisher of our faith.

INTRODUCTION

My life is in a pandemic, and it is not because of COVID-19. It feels like I am always making the same mistake, repeatedly putting my faith in people who seem to always let me down. This roller-coaster ride has created a lot of anxiety and emotional instability in my life. Normally, I am a peaceful, laid-back person, where nothing seems to rattle me. Oh, by the way, I failed to tell you that I am also a pastor. Trying to pastor a church was never something in life that I set out to do. It has caused me to have some personal pandemics. How do I please God while still trying to make others happy?

What is a pandemic? Well, this word means an event in which a disease spreads across several countries and affects many people. But it can also mean a crisis that affects every aspect of our lives that causes us to lose hope. How do we keep a level head of faith in tough times?

There are many kinds of pandemics in life: health, financial, spiritual, marital, loss of a loved one, and a coronavirus that can cause a worldwide pandemic.

My personal pandemic began several years ago. It was in August of 2015. The weather outside was sunny and warm as I remember it so well. I felt great as I started my day. I got an unexpected phone call from my doctor that there was something in one of my labs that made her suspicious. I was informed that my PSA reading was higher than the previous year before. Thinking it was probably nothing to be too concerned about, I went on with my normal pastoral duties. I got another call from my doctor a few days later, informing me that I needed to make an appointment with a urologist right away. I said to myself that I did not have time for this. My wife and I had an anniversary in a few weeks and a much-needed vacation planned to visit New York City. What could possibly be the problem? It was just probably a precautionary measure.

I had always been in good physical condition as a younger man. I played semiprofessional football, high school basketball and tennis, coached basketball, and little league football. I didn't drink alcohol or smoke cigarettes. I was a healthy guy. What was the big deal? Days later, I made an appointment to see this urologist as my doctor suggested. He did some further testing and discovered that I had prostate cancer. I was shocked and in denial. I remember thinking maybe someone was playing a bad joke on me, but I was not laughing. Was this really happening to me? My first test of a real crisis had just begun.

My mind began to wonder and question God, *How could you allow this to happen to me?* I was now faced with a health pandemic. How do you respond when the doctor delivers bad news? When your son or daughter has been brutally murdered? When your husband or wife wants to file for a divorce? When a deadly disease enters your body?

In this book, I want to help you discover how you can answer some of life's most challenging questions. I found my answer from the inspired Word of the LORD.

Discovering God's perspective on how you can answer some of life's most challenging questions is why I wrote this book!

PRELUDE INTRODUCTION

The year was 2019. There was a stranger that flew into the midst of our atmosphere. He attained permission to travel from city to city, state to state, and country to country. He was given permission to kill, steal, and destroy. This created havoc all over the world. At this time, no one knew his name and the effect he would have in our lives. He was an invisible enemy, an agent sent from the depths of hell to buffet our society and to change the way we think, work, and live. He came in quietly, unannounced, as a thief in the night with a bite that was much louder than his bark.

In January 2020 (the year of clear vision), our government was given information about this stranger but ignored its potential. For the first three months while this enemy was raging, our faith-based organizations had no knowledge of the harm this enemy could produce. Christians continued walking by faith and not by sight and trusting GOD according to his Word.

THERE WILL BE A PHRASE THROUGHOUT THIS BOOK THAT WE WILL CONTINUE TO ACKNOWLEDGE: "NOTHING HAPPENS ON EARTH UNLESS IT HAS HEAVEN'S PERMISSION."

This stranger was given the name coronavirus, COVID-19. This deadly virus became so devastating that to stop its deadly spread, state and local governments began to shutter all nonessential businesses. Even hospitals stopped all elective surgeries to make room for the many incoming infected patients. The world had to shelter in place. In over a century, America and the entire world hadn't experienced a pandemic quite like this. We were in another PANDEMIC.

Keeping a Level Head of Faith

Faith would be scrutinized and tested on all fronts. Friends, family members, churchgoers, and even believers began to suspect one another of being carriers of this deadly disease. Pastors and believers started to question God. But God would also begin to take notice of the stance Christians chose to take. What does the Scripture tell us to do in times like these? Are we to seek the advice of wise council and wisdom from the world, or do we search the scriptures for the truth of GOD's Word? This is not the time to add or take anything away from God's Word to appease our personal thoughts and decisions. In the apostle Paul's second letter to Timothy, it says, "Study to shew thyself approved unto God, a workman that needeth not to be ashamed, rightly dividing the word of truth" (2 Timothy 2:15). For us to do this, we must be willing to first deny ourselves and then take up the cross of Christ (Matthew 16:24).

Nothing Occurs to God: "Nothing Happens on Earth Unless It Has Heaven's Permission"

During this pandemic, representatives of God were not given the same opportunities to minister as other essential workers who were allowed to work on the front lines. It became frustrating not being able to perform my God-given responsibilities. The last time I checked, it was God that created the heavens and the earth and appointed holy representatives. "Moreover, whom He did predestinate, them He also called: and whom He called, them He also justified: and whom He justified, them He also glorified" (Romans 8:30).

I appreciate every person who has been given the burden of necessity to operate in the field in which they were predestined to be. The Lord has uniquely equipped those whom he has called and ordained to preach the Gospel, heal the sick, and cast out devils (Mark 3: 14–15).

Made for This Moment

Those that have been given this power: pastors, preachers, bishops, and evangelists, God is depending on us to work on the front line of defense against this enemy. I know there are moments we experience spiritual exhaustion, fear, and discouragement and think we can take shortcuts. But disobedience to God can result in serious consequences. God must be heard at times like these.

This stranger is no longer a stranger, COVID-19. It is time to issue him an eviction notice to vacate the premises. So I exhort all believers to hold fast to the faithful Word of God so that we may remain steadfast and unmovable always, abounding in the work of the Lord, knowing that our labor is not in vain in the Lord (1 Corinthians 15:58). "It's praying time"

PHASE 1

Laying the Foundation

Therefore thus saith the Lord God, Behold, I lay in Zion for a foundation a stone, a tried stone, a precious corner stone, a sure foundation: he that believeth shall not make haste.

—Isaiah 28: 16

Our world has changed drastically. What we have experienced is a disease that has created complete chaos and panic. As we try to wrap our minds around how to fix this situation, normally, we revert to human logic. Remember our theme, "nothing happens on earth unless it has heaven's permission." In the book of Job, the writer, who is assumed to be Moses, walked the back roads of the desert and ran into a man named Job who God would further use for his purpose. Job feared God and eschewed evil. Moses says in Job 1:6–8, "When the sons of God came to present themselves before the LORD, and Satan came also among them. The LORD then said unto Satan, 'Hast thou considered my servant Job, that there is none like him in the earth, he is a perfect and upright man.'" In the Bible, Job was a man of unfailing faith. Through trials and tribulations, he suffered great loss, but his faith in God never wavered. This is a perfect biblical example for us to follow during these challenging times.

This pandemic was not an accident but through the divine providence of God. Because of the refusal of man to obey God and repent from his sinful nature, heaven allowed this pandemic to happen. In the book of Matthew, Jesus preaches the greatest sermon that has ever been preached. He makes this profound statement in Matthew 5:18, "For verily I say unto you, till heaven and earth pass, one jot or one tittle shall in no wise pass from the law, till all be fulfilled." In the biblical times of the Mosaic Law, God's people would not change their ways. As we experience this pandemic today, many in the body of Christ have not changed their wicked ways. And until this happens, fulfilment cannot be achieved. *George Barna wrote, and I quote: "Jesus didn't die so we could fill auditoriums, he died so that lives could be transformed!"*

The Importance of Faith

The Bible teaches that faith is the key element in attaining eternal life in heaven with Christ, and because of this importance, Paul tells us in the book of Romans, "God have dealt every man a measure of faith." We all have an equal opportunity to build upon our measure of faith.

What is faith?

As a noun, *faith* is defined as complete trust or confidence in someone or something. Synonymous words: *belief, trust,* and *confidence. Faith* from a biblical perspective is defined as believing in the divine principles of the Gospel of Jesus Christ, his death, his burial, and, most importantly, his resurrection from death. Faith is the substance of things hoped for, the evidence of things not seen. If you must see it before you believe it, that is not faith. What does this really mean? It is a core basis of an unseen subfloor, which supports the very existence of our walk with God. For no man has ever seen God, but he has left us with this undisputable trail of evidence that results in our belief in him.

It is vitally important to establish a relationship with God. The scriptures declare that "without faith it is impossible to please him: for he that cometh to God must believe that he is, and that he is a rewarder of them that diligently seek him." (Hebrews 11:6). Therefore, when we are building our faith, we must diligently seek to learn of God. In return, we establish a relationship with God, knowing God comes with many rewards, including provisions and protection even during a pandemic. Faith is the substance of things "hoped for"—the presupposition is you cannot have faith…unless you have hope! Can we trust the inerrancy of the Bible—the literal nature of biblical accounts, especially regarding Christ's miracles and the creation account of Genesis, the virgin birth of Christ, the bodily resurrection and physical return of Christ, and the substitutionary atonement of Christ on the cross? These all require faith. Remember, what you believe will determine your final destiny.

During this COVID-19 pandemic, church attendance has drastically declined. Many Christians choose to stay at home because of their fear of this dreadful disease. Their faith began to fall allowing fear to rise. Believers find it hard to breathe, and God's people have begun to panic. *Christian researcher George Barna stated, "One in three practicing Christians or 32% has stopped attending church during this pandemic."*

This is one of many times in my pastoral assignment that I was challenged to take a stronger stance on the principles of God's Word despite monumental opposition. I heard the voice of the Almighty God say to me, *You are made for this very moment.* The doors of our church remained opened and because of this obedience to God, fourteen souls were added to the body of Christ, and four had been baptized. I might also note that we followed the recommended CDC guidelines. We are all soldiers in the army of the Lord. The Lord showed me that I cannot abandon my post. I believe that the sovereignty of God has compelled those to see him while staring down the barrel of this unseen enemy.

Best-selling author John Maxwell said, "A crisis does not make you a leader. A crisis reveals the need for leadership."

We need more leaders to emerge in difficult times—people who learn to triumph over adversity and become overcomers. Belief in our own ability can sometimes become a deterrent. It is not what you know but who you know. Jesus said in 1 John 5:5, "Who is he that overcometh the world, but he that believeth that Jesus is the Son of God?" The beautiful thing about leaders is their desire to serve the need of others. Sometimes, we need to step out of our own shadow of fear and know that a shadow can never hurt you. "Yea though I walk through the valley of the shadow of death, I will fear no evil: for thou art with me" (Psalm 23:4). We are not alone; God is always with us. So when leaders lead, the people will follow.

To encourage my congregation, the Lord spoke to me. He told me to teach a seven-week systematic class entitled "*Keeping a Level Head of Faith*." I was then given seven foundational scriptures to teach. In this chapter, we will learn that sturdiness of every house is subject to its foundation. We will be using parallels between that of a physical house and the building of a spiritual house. Remember, you cannot build a house without first laying its foundation. The building materials that you use to build your foundation will determine its life span.

"Teach me your way Lord and lead me to a level path" (Psalm 27:11).

In the familiar fairy tale "The Three Little Pigs," one built his house with straw, another built his with sticks, and the last one built his with bricks. During their lives, they came across an enemy called the big bad wolf who we will refer to as Satan. During his attack, he huffed and puffed and blew the first little piggy's straw house down. The little piggy then scrambled to his brother's house made of sticks. As the story goes, the big bad wolf huffed and puffed and blew the second piggy's house down. The two brothers scrambled to the third little piggy's house that was built with bricks. The big bad wolf huffed and puffed but could not blow the house made with bricks down.

The essence of this story is that we have an enemy that wants to blow down our spiritual houses and create havoc upon our lives. But if our spiritual lives are built on the solid foundation of Christ, the enemy cannot succeed. The Bible says in Ephesians 6:12, "For we wrestle not against flesh and blood, but against principalities, against powers, against the rulers of the darkness of this world, against spiritual wickedness in high places." *Remember it's not a me fight but rather a we fight.*

Nothing Happens on Earth Unless It Has Heaven's Permission

Faith is believing in the unseen, moving forward, and trusting that God has already paved the way to navigate us through these uncertain times.

The first of the seven systematic scriptures is in the book of Isaiah, one of my favorite Old Testament books. To keep a level head of faith, you must build upon the right foundation. The structure of every building requires a solid foundation. Without it, the building could suffer from stress cracks, which could ultimately cause serious external and internal damage.

Faith in Christ is the foundation that stabilizes our spiritual house. When we leave it unattended, it suffers from stress and mental fatigue and is subject to collapse. Jesus, while preaching his Sermon on the Mount, gives us the essence of having a sure foundation in Matthew 7.

As part of Jesus's Sermon on the Mount, in Matthew 7:24–27, he tells the story of two builders who lived in the same area. One built his house upon sand while the other built his house upon the rock. The meaning of the story is, as soon as the storms began raging in his life, the one that built his house on sand began to sink. You cannot build your house based on your bank account, your job, or family because this is not a sure foundation. You must build your house upon the solid foundation of Jesus Christ, so when the rains, floods, and winds come in your life, which are the different challenges of life, you will not sink, but you will be able to stand in the midst of the storm.

Also, in this same passage of scripture, Jesus says, "Therefore, whosoever heareth these sayings of mine, and doeth them, I will liken unto him a wise man that built his house upon a rock." Unfortunately, today there are many churchgoers that hear the Word of God every Sunday and at Wednesday night Bible studies but never do what the Word says. It is important to hear the sayings of Jesus, but what is more important is that we obey them.

In my earlier years of life while growing up, I always took a liking to world geography and history. I found it fascinating learning about our past. As I grew older, it became more apparent that I needed to take a deeper look into the foundation of our world and how it was built. Life has its personal questions that need to be answered. As I began my personal journey, I stumbled across a book in the Bible that bore my name called the book of Isaiah.

The book of Isaiah contains sixty-six chapters and is considered as the fifth Gospel because it contains prophecies of the birth of Jesus Christ. The theme of this book is salvation.

So within the saturated soil of our foundation, the most important part in Isaiah 28:16 is what you believe. You have probably heard the term you are what you eat. Well, let me say it this way: You are what you believe. To build the right spiritual foundation, we must believe in the infallible Word of God.

The prophet Isaiah had a threefold purpose: He first confronted his own nation and other contemporary nations with the Word of the Lord, concerning their sin and God's upcoming judgment. Second, he was given revelatory visions, the spirit of prophecy and hope to hold together the future generation of Jewish exiles. Finally, Isaiah prophesied that God was going to send his son, Jesus The Messiah, who would provide salvation, hope, and security to all that believed in him.

Now, let us explore our first fundamental foundational scripture. "Therefore thus saith the Lord God, Behold, I lay in Zion for a foundation a stone, a tried stone, a precious corner stone, a sure foundation: he that believeth shall not make haste" (Isaiah 28:16). As you can see, the word *stone* is used in three different ways in this scripture. This can be synonymous with the Trinity. The *stone* is the Lord himself. Faith in him provides hope for salvation. Zion refers to Jerusalem and not the church. The phrase *I lay in Zion for a foundation* is the first stage or phase in building your spiritual house, "laying this foundation."

The *Lord God* uses the superlative; *tried* it implies that this Stone is not an ordinary Stone. It is a tried Stone, meaning that many people have tried to tear down this Stone. Then the Lord says, it is a *precious Stone.* You cannot find this Stone in a rock quarry. This Stone was placed on the cross of Calvary to shed his precious blood for the sin of the world. He was beaten, bruised, and battered. He is a *sure* Stone. Christ was the same Stone that was seen in the fiery furnace with the three Hebrew boys in Daniel 3. Christ can only be a sure foundation to those who believe. If you believe in this Stone, you will not be stricken with panic.

There is value in this Stone. Time and pressure can cause the best of men to break, but with this Stone, the pressure is shifted from you and placed upon him. First

Peter 5:7 teaches us to cast all your care upon him for he cares for you. So let us cast our cares on the Lord and trust in the only One who can sustain our spiritual house upon his foundation.

Maintaining Your Spiritual Stability

In the process of building a physical house, one of the most important pieces is the cornerstone. The cornerstone is the part of the building that maintains the rest of the building. "Remember, what you believe can change your eternal destiny."

As we continue to reference the scriptures, we are taken to the apostle Paul's letter to the church at Ephesus. This will give us an internal view of the spiritual structure of our building. In Ephesians 2:20 (KJV), Paul says, "And are built upon the foundation of the apostles and prophets, Jesus Christ himself being the chief corner stone." This part of our study, "keeping a level head of faith," emphasizes that the foundation of the apostles and prophets originated from the inspiration of God. Paul further says how God inspired the prophets and apostles of old to write and record his Word. "All scripture is given by inspiration of God, and is profitable for doctrine, for reproof, for correction, for instruction, in righteousness: That the man of God may be perfect, thoroughly furnished unto all good works" (2 Timothy 3:16–17). The word *inspiration* that the apostle Paul uses here means that God anointed holy men and women to record his Word so that his Word has now become spiritually sanctified instead of physically motivated.

The apostle James, the half brother of Jesus, says it this way in James 1:22–25,

> But be ye doers of the word, and not hearers only, deceiving your own selves. For if any be a hearer of the word, and not a doer, he is like unto a man beholding his natural face in a glass: For he beholdeth himself, and goeth his way, and straightway forgetteth what manner of man he was.

James sums it up by saying,

> But whoso looketh into the perfect law of liberty, and continueth therein, he being not a forgetful hearer, but a doer of the work, this man shall be blessed in his deed.

James teaches us that when we examine our spirits and see our own shortcomings, we should not ignore them but do something to help build up our spiritual house. This could require more personal Bible study, prayer, and commitment to God.

To recap, Jesus is simply saying that *anyone who believes in me must not only hear my sayings but must become a doer of them.* Turning a deaf ear can be very dangerous.

"God is our refuge and strength…a very present help in trouble."

Christ's sayings are "solid" (Matthew 16:18) and "sanctified" (1 Peter 1:16), "provides security" (John 10:28), "saves" (Romans 10:9), and "seals" (Ephesians 4:30).

"For it is by Grace ye are saved through faith and that not of yourselves: it is the gift of God" (Ephesians 2:8).

Let us always remember the words of the prophet Isaiah: "Thus saith the Lord God, Behold, I lay in Zion for a foundation a stone, a *tried* stone, a *precious* corner stone, a *sure* foundation: he that believeth shall not make haste [or panic]."

In the book of 1 Corinthians 3:11, the apostle Paul gives us no other outlet. He emphasizes that Christ is the only way: "For other foundation can no man lay than that is laid, which is Jesus Christ." Jesus must be the center of attraction and be number one in our lives. In what is known as the center scripture of the Bible, Psalm 118:8 says these words: "It is better to trust in the Lord than to put confidence in man."

Calvary was not an accident. It was intentional. They hung Jesus on a cross, with a criminal on his right and another one on his left. However, the people did not come for the sideshow. They came for the main event—the man in the middle, who died for the sins of the world. He then rose on the third morning with all power in his hands. I believe this world has been given a wake-up call, and God is waiting for us to answer. In these challenging times, the only answer is, we must lay our spiritual foundation upon Christ Jesus. He alone must be the centerpiece of our lives.

PHASE 2

Building the Walls upon Our Foundation

The Lord is my rock and my fortress, my deliverer; my God, my strength, in whom will I trust; my buckler, and the horn of my salvation, and my high tower.

—Psalm 18:2

Now that the foundation has been laid in phase one, the next step is building the walls of our spiritual house upon this "solid foundation." When building a physical house, it is important that you select the appropriate building materials for the framing and erecting the walls. God has divinely chosen our spiritual materials that will be needed for the framing and strengthening of our spiritual house. God is omniscient (meaning all-knowing). He knows the dates, directions, and darts of demonic influences that Satan will use to try to tear your spiritual house down. REMEMBER, NOTHING HAPPENS ON EARTH UNLESS IT HAS HEAVEN'S PERMISSION.

Many of us were going through a personal pandemic when the coronavirus invaded the land. I would like to share some of my personal story. Satan tried to discourage me because of my personal health issues. I was diagnosed with cancer in 2015. Before deciding to take the advice of my physical doctors, I prayed and asked God for healing. During one of my personal prayer sessions, I felt a cold drop of water hit the back of my neck. This water appeared to come from above. It chilled my body, and I immediately felt physically different. My first thought was, *Is this a sign from God?* I looked up at the ceiling to try to determine where the water came from. To my astonishment, there was no way that water could have fallen from the ceiling. I did not have any leaks in my roof. How could this have happened?

I knew this was an extraordinary moment. The first sign was, I had been experiencing a tremble in my left thumb from a recent procedure. The trembling in my thumb stopped immediately. I then noticed the pain in my back that I have been suffering with for many years immediately stopped, and I had not had any back pain since this experience. I was asymptomatic with the cancer; therefore, I cannot say that I felt any physical difference in my body from the cancer. I can tell you I felt the healing power of

God, which made my entire body feel better. This was a moment of epiphany for me.

I WAS HEALED, but trying to prove this to others was the biggest obstacle I would face. My doctors would deny me another test to justify my beliefs. I was told that I still needed those forty-three radiation treatments.

I asked God, "Why do I need to take the radiation treatments?"

The answer that I got did not make sense to me at that time.

He said, *It is not for you, but for me.*

Still trusting God and obeying his Word, I started the treatments because God said, *Just do it.*

After a few weeks, I started to see what my purpose was for being there. Many others that were being treated for different types of cancer began to show up around the time that my appointments would be scheduled.

I asked one of the nurses, "Why are all these people here at the same time?

I knew that all of us could not have the same appointment times. She told me that most of them were staying after their treatment was done to speak to me.

I gave them encouragement from God's Word. A lot of these patients were extremely sick. They needed to hear from the Lord. It was the faith that I demonstrated in the Lord that was able to impart spiritual strength into their lives. This helped them during this frightening time in their lives. Their faith was now being developed. *At that moment, I understood what God told me: It's not for you, but it is for me.*

His Grace Was Being Made Sufficient

In December 2019, just before the pandemic, I went to my doctor for a regular checkup. And to my astonishment, my numbers were high again. In January of 2020, I was referred to a specialist. He performed further tests and confirmed that my cancer had returned and showed signs that it had metastasized.

God reminded me THAT HIS GRACE IS SUFFICIENT, even in my physical weakness.

By the grace of God, I continued to move forward in my ministry. At that time, I did not want this news to become public. The congregation was already dealing with enough challenges because of the pandemic. I only shared this information with a few of my staff members. I had to remain steadfast and unmovable because I knew my labor would not be in vain.

Dealing with a Private Pandemic and Now a Public Pandemic

Psalm 18:2 is a psalm of King David where he spoke unto the LORD the words of this song in the day of deliverance while on the run from Saul and all his enemies. He used eight stanzas that identify who the LORD was to him.

We will use these eight stanzas as the strength and stability for building our spiritual walls in the midst of a pandemic. In biblical numerology, the number eight represents new beginnings, so while we are framing our spiritual houses, we must also apply these same stanzas. Firstly, the LORD is "my rock," which means he is my foundation. David uses the personal name of the LORD, which is Yahweh or Jehovah.

Secondly, "my fortress" means mountain or stronghold, a place of strength and safety. The Hebrew name for *fortress* is *Maw-tsood,* which means a net, capture, a fastness, castle of defense, or fort. Our spiritual houses are now structured like a fort or castle of defense that pushes back enemy forces. In battling against deadly pandemics, we can never lower our spiritual walls.

Nothing occurs to God; he knows all things. When trouble arises, everyone needs a place to retreat. Whenever Moses came upon trouble with the children of Israel, he would retreat to his HIGH MOUNTAIN, "which means God." When Christ would face tough times, having to make decisions concerning the kingdom, he would retreat to his MOUNTAIN, "which means God" (Exodus 19:3, Matthew 14:23, Mark 6:46, and Luke 6:12). When this pandemic invaded our land, Christians needed to retreat to God. He is our fortress.

The third stanza, "my deliverer," means living protector. The Hebrew word *paw-lat* means to slip out, escape, or carry away safely. Let us think of it this way: With Christ as the foundation, God is building a new people whose commitment must be to righteousness and justice. Psalm 118:17 says, "I shall not die, but live, and declare the works of the Lord." Verse twenty-two goes on to say, "The stone which the builders refused is become the head stone of the corner." This teaches us that the walls of our spiritual houses are made with the stone of Jesus Christ. With his protection, it makes our walls much harder for the enemy to tear down.

The fourth stanza says "my God." The Hebrew name for God is *Elohim,* which means three strong and mighty ones. It is always in its plural form, which represents the Trinity. This should remind us that there is nothing impossible when you have the omnipotence of God working on your behalf.

In the fifth stanza David says "my strength," which means he is immovable. His power is unmatchable.

The sixth stanza says "my buckler," which means a shield. This symbolizes that God comes between us and harm. The apostle Paul says it this way in Ephesians 6:16, "Above all, taking the shield of Faith, wherewith ye shall be able to quench all the fiery darts of the wicked." This is our defense from the enemy that tries to destroy us.

The seventh stanza, "horn of my salvation," symbolizes power, kingship, a mighty salvation, or a strong savior. In biblical numerology, the number seven means "completion and perfection." In 1 Thessalonians 4:16–17, the apostle Paul says:

> For the Lord himself shall descend from heaven with a shout, with the voice of the archangel, and with the trump of God: and the dead in Christ shall rise first. Then we which are alive shall be caught up together with them in the clouds, to meet the Lord in the air; and so shall we ever be with the Lord.

This is the "sound of satisfaction," knowing that Christ will no longer rely on his prophets and apostles. He carries the "horn of salvation" that all believers will hear whether you are dead in the grave and or still alive.

The eighth and final stanza of David's song to the LORD says "my high tower," which signals a place so high that danger cannot reach you. Here God becomes personal to David. He uses the pronoun *my* eight times in this passage of the scripture. As the saying goes, "when our feet strike Zion," the new Jerusalem, the new heaven, and the new earth, this will be our new beginning. In order to be a part of this new beginning, just as David did, you must establish a personal relationship with God.

So now, let us reflect on the second foundational scripture in Psalm 18:2. David shows us that God creates a safehouse for us, giving us his protection always. Isaiah gives us further assurance when he says in Isaiah 54:17, "No weapon that is formed against thee shall prosper; and every tongue that shall rise against thee in judgment thou shalt condemn. This is the heritage of the servants of the Lord, and their righteousness is of me, saith the Lord."

Just as your physical house needs electric power, your spiritual house needs the power of God to function properly. God, in his infinite wisdom, has given every believer a measure of faith. We must build upon this faith and try not to allow our faith to fall to the point that we become weak. This is when we began to experience fear and panic. At these times, you must seek God for the cleansing and replenishing of our physical and spiritual strength. Fear creates doubt, and some of the greatest faith patriots throughout the Bible had experienced moments where it seemed as though God was not present.

So as we move forward, let us be reminded that when God is silent, we must be still. As Moses said to the people in Exodus 14:13, "Do not be afraid. Stand still, and see the salvation of the Lord, which He will accomplish for you today. For the Egyptians whom you see today, you shall see again no more forever. The Lord will fight for you, and you shall hold your peace."

"NEVER ALLOW FEAR TO RENT A ROOM IN YOUR SPIRITUAL CASTLE." Keep reminding yourself that "greater is HE that is in me than he that is in the world" (1 John 4:4). Build up your wall of faith on the solid foundation of Jesus Christ.

PHASE 3

Installing the Insulation for Our Spiritual Walls

And the Lord, he it is that doth go before thee; he will be with thee, he will not fail thee, neither forsake thee: fear not, neither be dismayed.

—Deuteronomy 31:8

The book of Deuteronomy is Moses's "swan song" that was written before his death. It contains the miraculous moments when God revealed himself to Moses, as well as the children of Israel. It should provide us with insulation and security, teaching us that God is always with us and nothing escapes him.

Although many of the patriarchs of the Old Testament demonstrated deep faith in God, the actual word *faith* only appears two times in the King James version of the Old Testament. It appears in the books of Deuteronomy and Habakkuk. The children of Israel displayed great faith when they followed Moses out of Egypt as he followed a God he had never seen. This same faith must be exemplified in every believer as this pandemic roars through our land. Before COVID-19 reached our shores, many Christians displayed what appeared to be an unshakeable faith in God. But as this pandemic spread, believers lost their spiritual vision, and they could no longer see with their spiritual sight but rather depended on their physical sight. Paul teaches us in 2 Corinthians 5:7 "For we walk by faith and not by sight."

When building a physical house, you will need a good construction manager. His job is to oversee the entire building project from start to finish. In this part of our faith-building process, we will refer to God as our construction manager. He can spot a potential problem in our life before it even becomes a real problem. When we put our faith in God and ask, he will go before us and provide assurance that our life's projects are on the right course.

In Deuteronomy 31, Moses portrays God as a warrior that goes before him and defeats and removes the debris from his path. At a construction site, there are always people that come by the site to visualize how the house will look when completed, to look for ideas for their projects, or just out of curiosity. Also, there are those who visit the site without good intentions. We will refer to them as thieves and robbers. They come along the construction site to try and steal or vandalize it. That is why security is so important at every construction site. Jesus warns us in John 10:10, "The thief cometh not, but for to steal, and to kill, and to destroy: I am come that they might have life, and that they might have it more abundantly."

To help us keep a level head of faith, our third foundational scripture, Deuteronomy 31:8, is a text of assurance, confirmation, accommodation, and reassurance. Moses says, "And the LORD, He it is that doth go before thee; He will be with thee, He will not fail thee, neither forsake thee: fear not, neither be dismayed." COVID-19 has created fear around the world. *Remember that nothing happens on earth unless it has heaven's permission.* God makes a threefold promise within this text: He will be with thee; he will not fail thee, neither forsake thee. Those were the three promises that God made to Moses and the children of Israel. Because all Christians are elects of God, these same promises apply to each of us.

During these times of uncertainty, we must remain focused on these very promises of God. Because God is omniscient, which means all-knowing, and nothing is unknown to him, even this pandemic had to have his permission. God can see around the curves and corners of life. There have been many times in our lives that God have gone before us and shielded us from some unknown danger. A great example of this is when the Egyptians and Pharaoh's army had trapped the Israelites between the mountains and the Red Sea. God shielded them with a pillar of fire behind them and parted the Red Sea that was in front of them so that they were able to walk across it on dry land, and the enemies that pursued after them were drowned in the midst of the sea.

Fear is an instrument used by Satan that causes one to be blinded of the promises of God's Word. Therefore, when installing the insulation of our spiritual walls, we are not to be afraid, neither be dismayed. Weapons will form, but they shall not prosper. Deuteronomy 31:7 says, "And Moses called unto Joshua, and said unto him in the sight of all Israel, be strong and of good courage; for thou must go with this people unto the land which the Lord hath sworn unto their fathers to give them; and thou shalt cause them to inherit it."

Even after Moses passed, God reassured Joshua. In the book of Joshua 1:5–6, it says:

> There shall not any man be able to stand before thee all the days of thy life: as I was with Moses, so I will be with thee: I will not fail thee; nor forsake thee. Be strong and of a good courage: for unto this people shalt thou divide for an inheritance the land, which I sware unto their fathers to give them.

Always remember, you are not alone. That which is placed in you, the "Holy Spirit," he will always provide comfort and security.

He Will Never Fail Thee

In the New Testament, as recorded in Hebrews 13:5, it says, "Let your conversation be without covetousness; and be content with such things as ye have: for he hath said [*meaning Jesus Christ*], I will never leave thee, nor forsake thee." Believers are assured that if they love God above all else and lean and depend on him and not to the material security of this world, the Lord will never desert them, but he will always be their guide.

Remember, our construction manager of our property is the Lord God. He is the one that goes before us to ensure our safety. Always consult your Manager before you proceed forward. God can analyze a situation a lot better than we can. According to Hebrews 12:2, we are told that "looking unto Jesus the author and finisher of our faith; who for the joy that was set before him endured the cross, despising the shame, and is set down at the right hand of the throne of God." He is the author, and he knows the conclusion of matter.

Faith in Christ is the antidote and the antibiotic for COVID-19 as well as many other unseen forces that oppose our belief system. Remember, we must not waiver. In Psalm 1:3, David said "that we ought to be like a tree that's planted by the rivers of water, that bringeth forth his fruit in his season; his leaf also shall not wither; and whatsoever he doeth shall prosper." In this season of COVID-19, David is letting us know that we must be like that tree planted by the rivers of water. We must not allow the fear of this deadly disease to overwhelm our root system. Fear can cause our leaves to wither, and we can become claustrophobic in our own homes. That is why, it is so important that we insulate our spiritual walls with faith in Jesus Christ.

We Are in Our Season

I can think back to my younger days when I played football in Omaha, Nebraska. I was blessed with the talent to play football. I played the position of halfback or running back. In this position, I loved to keep the defense confused when I ran the football. This created fear within them and would throw them off their game. Only playing defense against this pandemic is throwing us off our purpose. This is a great time to exhibit our faith in GOD. We are not only to be defensive Christians but also must use the gift of being offensive Christians.

The Word of God is our weapon of power. In Deuteronomy 31:8 (eight being the number of new beginnings), it is time for us to begin our offense against this virus. In this foundational scripture, "And the LORD" is not just a phrase. It identifies his covenant name, Yehowah. It is most prominently known in connection with his relationship with the nation of Israel. It was a firm tradition by the Jews to never pronounce his most holy name. They generally substituted it with something else. But today, believers casually use his name, not really understanding the significant power behind the name LORD.

He is the accommodation of assurance in the Old Testament. Deuteronomy 31:8 goes on to say, "He it is that doth go before thee." Our lives have already been pre-planned or predestined by God. The prophet Jeremiah says it this way, "The LORD said; "Before I formed thee in the belly, I knew thee; and before thou camest forth out of the womb I sanctified thee, and I ordained thee a prophet unto the nations" (Jeremiah 1:5).

In the Hebrew syntax "go before thee," the LORD is saying here that there is no reason for us to walk in fear, although we may not know what lies ahead of us. He has already paved the way for our journey and set the course of our destination. In this text, the word *go* in its original form is *Halakh*, which means *to walk, go,* or *come*. This lets us know he has given us a *promise of protection*. As we dig deeper into this text, it says, "He will be with thee; he will not fail thee." The Hebrew word for *fail* is *Raphah*, which means *to be slack, to be remiss,* or *to be idle*. He gives his *promise of prevailing*.

The LORD goes on to say, "Neither forsake thee."

The word *forsake* in Hebrew is *Azav* meaning *to loosen, relinquish,* or *release to permit; to set free; to leave, forsake, abandon,* or *leave behind; to omit; to relax;* or *to be forsaken*.

Here, the LORD has *procured security* for us. This means that he will always take care of us. He will never abandon or leave us behind.

The Lord goes on to say, "Fear not."

What the LORD is telling us is that we must be *persistent* in our faith because he has told us to fear not.

Finally, the Lord says, "Neither be dismayed."

We are to never allow the circumstances around our world to overwhelm us, to crush or bruise our faith, to break our spirit, nor to alarm our inner soul to cause confusion in our lives.

The National Association for Stock Car Auto Racing (NASCAR) always has something called the pace car. This car is sent out first. This is done to check the track for any obstructions, bad weather, or any other safety obstacles. This procedure protects all the other cars that are participating in the race. The LORD is the pace car that "goes out before us" to make sure that our *pathway to prosperity* in heaven has been made perfect for us.

Philippians 3:13–14 says, "Brethren, I count not myself to have apprehended: but this one thing I do, forgetting those things which are behind, and reaching forward unto those things which are before, I press toward the mark for the prize of the High calling of God in Christ Jesus." As we go through this pandemic, keep your eyes on the prize of Christ Jesus. Only insulate your spiritual walls with unwavering faith in him.

PHASE 4

Attaining Our Permit

For God hath not given us the spirit of fear; but of power, and of love, and of a sound mind.

—2 Timothy 1:7

In this building process, we must attain a permit to give fear an eviction notice.

We have now reached the center scripture in our quest for perfection and completion. In biblical numerology, the number seven represents perfection and completion. Therefore, our fourth foundational scripture is vitally important because it provides the balance to the number seven by placing three scriptures before it and three scriptures after it. This has led us to an epiphany (a manifestation of a divine or supernatural being) of Christ by shining an additional light onto our lives.

As we continue to keep our level head of faith during this pandemic, we turn to the apostle Paul. Paul has been attributed to the writing of thirteen books in the New Testament. It is interesting to note that Paul wrote his second letter to Timothy from a Roman prison while he was awaiting his own impending death. This is one of the greatest demonstrations of his faith, not allowing the fear of death to overwhelm his spiritual thinking. *Remember, nothing happens on earth unless it has heaven's permission.* Timothy was one of the apostle Paul's spiritual sons in the Gospel. The reason for this letter to Timothy was because Paul knew that due to false doctrine, Timothy would face many oppositions within the New Testament church.

In phase 4 of our quest to keep a level head of faith, we journey to 2 Timothy 1:7, "For God hath not given us the spirit of fear; but of power, and of love, and of a sound mind." Let us first see what God has given the believers: He gives us a trinitarian package that contains first, the spirit of power; second, the spirit of love; and third, the spirit of a sound mind. But remember, there is a stranger that lurks around our spiritual house, trying to gain access and cause fear. On the surface, it looks as though this stranger is no match against our trinitarian power. But when we fall under great pressure from this stranger, we can succumb to its power, which can cause us to sin against God.

Let us look at the word *fear*. It is interesting in this text that *fear* is identified as she. The meaning of the Greek word *fear* in this text is *Delila* or better known as Delilah;

it means cowardice, timidity, fearfulness, or to flee from or run away from. If God did not give you a measure of fear, then where did it come from? In the Old Testament book of Judges, there was an Israelite named Samson, who followed the proscription (the act of forbidding or banning something) of Nazirite life, which included not drinking or trimming his hair. He was a man of tremendous strength that was given to him from God.

Delilah was a central figure of Samson's last love story (Judges 16:15–17). She was a Philistine woman who was bribed to entrap Samson. She coaxed him into revealing that the secret of his strength was his long hair. While he slept, the faithless Delilah brought in a Philistine who cut Samson's hair, draining his strength. Please note that his strength came from the power of God. (Judges 14:6, 15:14). If Delilah can create fear, she then can drain you of your strength and power just as she did with Samson.

The apostle Paul was warning Timothy that there would be some Delilahs in the church that could steal your spirit of power, your spirit of love, and your spirit of a sound mind. Delilah is no more than an agent of Satan, summoned to create doubt, fear, anxiety, stress, and delusion in our lives. This can cause us to oppose God's Word. I believe that fear was given permission from God to try our faith in the form of COVID-19. So during this pandemic, we cannot allow fear to take our power away.

Since this spirit of fear "COVID-19" has been exposed, we can now use our "spirit of power" to conquer this enemy.

The Greek word for *power* here is *Dunamis*. It is where we get our English word *dynamite* meaning this power is especially inherited. It is a supernatural power that can destroy any enemy that wages war against us. This comes from God, and Satan is no match for the power of God. We now know we have the power to detonate any fear that the enemy tries to throw our way. *Remember, nothing happens on earth unless it has heaven's permission. God has power over COVID-19.*

Now we know the first arsenal in our trinitarian package, "spirit of power," is working on our behalf. Let's look at the "spirit of love." The word *love* in this passage of scripture is *Agape*. This is a Greco-Christian term meaning benevolent love, the highest form of love. This love is not shown by doing what the person that you love desires but what you deem as needed for the one that you love. In John 3:16, God showed us the ultimate benevolence: "God so loved the world that he gave his only begotten son." Here, God gave man not what man wanted but what man needed (Jesus was rejected by his own people). God perceived man's need for forgiveness of sins when he sacrificed his Son, Jesus Christ. God has given us the love that has the power to fight fear or Delilah. The Bible teaches us in 1 John 4:18, *"there is no fear in love; but perfect love casteth out fear: because fear hath torment. He that feareth is not made perfect in love."* For an example, just as when one goes fishing, he cast his line as far out as he can from the shore. God has given us the power to cast fear away from us as far as we can. If you find yourself surrounded by others who have been overtaken by fear, this can weaken your spirit and power. But you can always use the spirit of love to cast away this negativity. The love of God can conquer all fear.

The third part of the trinitarian power that the apostle Paul gave to Timothy was the "spirit of a sound mind." The Greek word here for a sound mind is *So-fron-is-mis*, which means discipline and self-control. It is a word that is given to us to help us think rationally and not irrationally. What may appear to be logical may not have any biblical substance to support it. God has given our government power according to Romans 13:1–5, but when that power is in contradiction of the Word of God, we must be able to use our spirit of a sound mind to defuse it. Our country is divided in many areas, such as religion, race, morals, and political views. As Christians, we must overcome these divisions based on the Word of God. It is our faith and not fear that makes us overcomers. First John 5:5 says, "Who is he that overcometh the world, but he that believeth that Jesus is the Son of God?"

It would be unfair at this point if I did not let you know that fear is a two-sided coin. The good side of fear will cause your love to grow into a deeper reverence and understanding of God. Isaiah 43:1b says, "Fear not; for I have redeemed thee, I have called thee by my name, you are mine." The good side of fear tells us we must revere God in all we do because he has made our lives possible. As Solomon declares in Ecclesiastes 12:13, "Let us hear the conclusion of the whole matter: Fear God, and keep his commandments for this is the whole duty of man." What this simply means is, we must love God and revere his Word by demonstrating obedience to his commandments because all our works will be brought into judgment whether they be good or bad.

In conclusion of phase 4, do not allow the circumstances of life to cause you to take your eyes off Jesus. When we are looking at fear, we cannot see Jesus because fear is of Satan, and God has given us the power to defeat fear. In the book of Matthew 14:22–33, Jesus constrained his disciples to get into a ship and to go before him unto the other side while he sent the multitude away. This occurred during the fourth watch (this is between the hours of 3:00 a.m. and 6:00 a.m.). As a mighty storm was raging on the sea, Jesus came to his disciples, walking upon the water. They were troubled, saying it was a spirit, and they cried out for fear.

But Jesus spoke out to them saying, "Be of good cheer; it is I; be not afraid."

Peter, being the boldest of the disciples, said, "Lord if it be thou, bid me to come unto thee on the water."

Jesus said, "Come."

And Peter responded by coming down out of the ship, and he began walking on the water. At this moment, Peter's faith defied the laws of gravity. Just as Jesus was standing on the water, Peter was walking on the water. But when he saw the wind become boisterous, he took his eyes off Jesus, and he became afraid and began to sink. The storms and winds of life can become a Delilah if you take your eyes off Jesus. So just remember, according to 2 Corinthians 11:14, "And no marvel for Satan himself is transformed into an angel of light." We have learned in phase 4 that we must always keep our mind, heart, soul, and sight on the true light of God.

We have made the case, and we have the permit to give fear an eviction notice.

PHASE 5

Adding Light to Our Spiritual Houses

The Lord is my light and my salvation; whom shall I fear? The LORD is the strength of my life; of whom shall I be afraid?

—Psalm 27:1

When building a physical house, the next building phase requires running electricity to the entire house by making what is called a series of "home runs." The term *home run wiring* in the building process consists of several "home runs" from a central distribution point to various places in the home. Each "home run" is a dedicated line that can provide the strongest possible signal to each device on the network.

Psalm 27:1 can be identified as our home run verse. This fifth systemic scripture signifies the act of God's grace, which is the gift of salvation.

Light Is the Pathway to Spiritual Strength and Freedom

Psalm 27:1 is a psalm of David's confidence in God: "The LORD is my light and my salvation; whom shall I fear? The LORD is the strength of my life; of whom shall I be afraid?" This scripture gives us a threefold purpose of the LORD, which is to provide light to our spiritual houses, salvation for our souls, and strength to our lives. With all these provisions from the Lord, the scripture asks the rhetorical question, "Whom shall I be afraid?" REMEMBER THIS STATEMENT: "NOTHING HAPPENS ON EARTH UNLESS IT HAS HEAVEN'S PERMISSION." As we can see, David begins to exhibit unwavering faith in God.

I learned at an early age the seriousness of life and death and the importance of seeking eternal life. This all started to resonate with me when I was a young boy growing up in Omaha, Nebraska. We lived near a funeral home, and out of curiosity of our youth, my three brothers and I would often go and view the remains of the dearly departed. There was something dark and gloomy about viewing lifeless bodies. These early experiences of seeing death had a profound effect on my life and made me appreciate the light of my salvation.

Also, when playing outside as children, whenever the streetlights came on, it allowed us to continue to play despite darkness. You could say, the darkness could not comprehend the light. John 1:4–5 says it this way, "In him was life; and the life was the light of men. And the light shineth in darkness; and the darkness comprehended it not." This scripture now starts to make sense to me because of some of the things that we were doing as little children. David had many moments of darkness, but he began to see God in the light and to appreciate his salvation.

In our foundational scripture, Psalm 27:1, the Hebrew word for *light* is *OR*. It means light, brightness, lighting, daylight, sunlight, illumination, enlightenment, happiness, and cheerfulness. Light is an important concept in the Bible whether literally or figuratively. It allows us to go left or right. This Hebrew word *OR* signifies life in contrast with death, as we can see in Psalm 56:13: "For thou hast delivered my soul from the death: wilt not thou deliver my feet from falling, that I may walk before God in the light of the living?"

What David understood is that God has no limitations. He can provide light when everything around us appears dark. He brings brightness in the midst of calamity. He is our power source of daylight, which is the sunlight. He is our illumination and enlightenment. He can open our spiritual conscience to his divine truth and expose the dark domains that Satan loves to operate in.

Satan has tried to cast a shadow of darkness in the lives of many of God's people, which can lead to depression. But as we can see from the word of God, our spiritual houses now have God's electricity flowing through them. Because of this light, we can experience happiness and cheerfulness in the midst of this pandemic. His Word awakens and brightens our paths. "The word is a lamp unto my feet and a light unto my path" (Psalm 119:105).

David said the Lord was his light and his salvation. Let us place emphasis on the word *salvation*. What would be the purpose for living a good life and die and then go to a burning hell? I rather live my life believing that there is a God than to die and then find out after death. When we think of the term *home run wiring*, salvation comes to mind. This is like hitting a home run. You get to run around all the bases without anyone impeding your path, and then as you cross home plate, the cheerfulness begins.

When Jesus died on the cross of Calvary for the sins of the world, he hit a home run, crushed Satan, and bruised his heel, but it wouldn't be until three days later that he would rise with all power in his hand. He now sits on the right hand of the Father, petitioning on our behalf.

Now let us define the word *salvation*. The Hebrew word *Ye' Sha* or *yesha* means liberty, deliverance, help, salvation, freedom, welfare, and prosperity. This powerful word carries a sevenfold blessing. Jesus's death on the cross supplied all our physical and spiritual needs. As Paul said in Philippians 4:19, "But my God shall supply all your need according to his riches in glory by Christ Jesus." Our need is never greater than his riches. "For he owns the cattle of a thousand hills. The silver and the gold belong to the Lord. The earth is the Lord's and the fullness thereof; the world, and they that dwell therein" (Psalm 50:10, Haggai 2:8, Psalm 24:1).

Security is only found in God's grace and mercy. So who shall we fear? Of whom shall we be afraid, and what possibly can shake our strength? God must be revered in all the earth.

While studying a few years ago, I came across Luke 12:4–5, and this scripture has stuck with me. The explanation of this scripture is, because God is the Creator of the heavens and the Earth, there is no one greater than him. The Bibles says, "And I say unto you my friends, be not afraid of them that kill the body, and after that have no more they can do. But I forewarn you whom ye shall fear: Fear him, which after he hath killed hath power to cast into hell; yea, I say unto you, Fear him" (Luke 12:4–5).

To keep a level head of faith in the midst of a pandemic, we must have the faith that David unleashed against the forces of evil. In conclusion of this phase, let us define the last part of our scripture: *"of whom shall I be afraid?"* The Hebrew word of *fear* is *Yare*. It means to be afraid, fear, or revere; to be feared; to be dreadful; to be revered; or to terrify and make afraid. This speaks of the spiritual side of fear, which only belongs to God. This can be a positive feeling or reverence for God that we can express through piety or in a formal manner.

But there is another type of fear that shows the emotional and intellectual anticipation of harm and the feeling that something terrible is about to happen. At these times, we must exhibit faith such as Peter in the book of Matthew. His faith allowed him to walk on water. Faith will plant your feet firmly on the foundation of Christ, and faith will give you an opportunity to magnify God even during a pandemic. You can never strike out with Christ as your designated hitter.

PHASE 6

Adding the Roof and Trusses on Our Spiritual Building

Trusting the Builder

Trust in the LORD with all thine heart; and lean not unto thine own understanding.

—Proverbs 3:5

The roof and truss are an essential part of building a physical home. This gives the home protection from the outside elements and provides privacy. As we try to keep a level head of faith during a pandemic, our sixth systemic scripture teaches us that we must lean and depend on God. We cannot depend on our own limited understanding; this only leads to trouble. In biblical numerology, six is the number of man. In five days, God created the heavens and the earth. And on the sixth day, he made man in his own image, male and female. He then rested on the seventh day.

God is our Creator; therefore, he knows what the future holds for us. I can look back when I was a young man. I was on a totally different path and thought, at the time, it was a great path. I enjoyed many hobbies: coaching and playing basketball, class A flag football and by the grace of God, Semi-pro football. I had a great job working at the Union Pacific Railroad and purchased a home in Omaha, Nebraska. I had a brand-new car and money in the bank. At this time, I really felt my future was laid out for me. All I needed to do was to stay the course. But in December of 1988, things started to change. The Union Pacific Railroad closed its doors in Omaha and offered everyone buyouts or an opportunity to continue working in another state. With my seniority, I decided to move to Little Rock, Arkansas, and further my railroad career. At the time, I was raising my two sons and later connected with my third son in Alabama.

I began to believe that this was my new path in life. God knew I was missing a helpmeet. I was not even looking for one, but God caused me to experience my own Cinderella story. I met the most beautiful woman named Cheryl. She had two children, a boy and a girl. Not long after meeting, we married and became a blended family. She is my rib and soul mate for life.

As we started to build a life together, I was called into the ministry and later to pastor God's sheep. This is when my life took a serious turn. I had no idea I would be pastoring a church, and God would provide me with a helpmeet for this great calling. We cannot lean on our own understanding; we must learn to trust God.

King Solomon, the writer of Proverbs, explained that our own understanding is limited, fallible, and subject to error. God's wisdom is quite extraordinary. He has predestined our lives to work harmoniously together with his plan. This is still true in the midst of this current pandemic. Proverbs 3:5 says, "Trust in the LORD with all thine heart; and lean not unto thine own understanding."

"Trust in the Lord" is a Hebrew syntax (this is a group of words that are combined to give us one meaning). When we think of the roof and trusses for a physical house, they must be strong and sturdy. There is no one that is stronger than God. We can feel complete comfort when we trust in the Lord. When we put our trust in the Lord, we receive the promises of the Lord, the protection of the Lord, and the provisions of the Lord. This gives us trinitarian power (power of the Trinity).

The Hebrew word for *trust* here is *Ba-Tach*. It means to attach oneself; to trust, confide in, feel safe, be confident, or secure or to be careless or "rely on." The basic idea here is associated with firmness in solidity. We are told to never put our complete trust in any humanistic association. Psalm 118:8 warns us, "It is better to trust in the Lord than to put confidence in man."

The Hebrew word *Ba-Tach* is where we derive our English word *attached*, which means joined, fastened, or connected to something. This teaches us that our mind and heart should only be joined, fastened, and connected to the LORD. When Solomon said, "Trust in the Lord with all thine heart," here, he is not referring to the physical heart, which pumps blood throughout the body. He is referring to the mainframe or our mind.

The Hebrew word here for *heart* is *Lev*. It means the totality of man's inner or immaterial nature. In the Bible, the whole spectrum of human emotion is attributed to the heart. It is also where wisdom and understanding reside. It is known as the seat of the will as Moses recorded in Numbers 16:28: "And Moses said, Hereby ye shall know that the Lord hath sent me to do all these works; for I have not done them of mine own mind."

The Lord now becomes the driver of our car, and we should become his passengers. And he does not need a back seat driver. The song written by Douglas Miller, "My Soul Has Been Anchored in the Lord," contains these lyrics: "When the storms keep on raging in my life and sometimes it's hard to tell the night from day, still that hope that lies within is reassured. As I keep my eyes upon the distant shore, I know He'll lead me safely to that blessed place He has prepared." The Lord is the only one that we can place our trust in. Only he can lead us to that distant shore. In the midst of this pandemic, the Lord must become our anchor.

Proverbs 3:5b says, "Lean not unto thine own understanding." We should no longer be driven by our own human intellect or understanding. Remember, our own understanding is limited, fallible, and subject to error. Ephesians 4:18 says it this way, "Having the understanding darkened, being alienated from the life of God through the ignorance that is in them because of the blindness of their heart." Not leaning on God can lead to darkness, alienation, and ignorance of what is right.

The Hebrew word for *lean* is *Sha`an*. This means to support oneself, lean against, or place confidence in someone or something. The Lord must become our support beam, and we must place all our confidence in him. He alone will give us rest. As we can see in Matthew 11:28–29, Christ said, "Come unto me, all ye that labor and are heavy laden, and I will give you rest. Take my yoke upon you, and learn of me; for I am meek and lowly in heart: and ye shall find rest unto your souls." Knowledge and understanding are vitally important.

What Jesus is saying here is, *Come to me during your problems; don't place your confidence and trust in man because man is not capable of carrying such a heavy load.* Jesus is graciously telling us to take a break and allow him to carry our load so that we can rest our minds from the burdens of this world. COVID-19 has become one of these heavy burdens he is speaking of. REMEMBER THE STATEMENT "NOTHING HAPPENS ON EARTH UNLESS IT HAS HEAVEN'S PERMISSION."

When I played basketball in high school, coach Gene Haynes would tell us, "Do not think when we are on the court." He further said, "That is why I am here to do the thinking for you."

Because as young boys, we tended to try to show off and do our own thing to impress the crowd, and this usually did not turn out well. God is telling us not to lean to our own understanding but allow him to do the thinking for us. If we take notice, every time we do not allow the Lord to lead us, the end results never turn out well.

Now let us deal with the word *understanding* in the passage. The Hebrew word for *understanding* is Bin`ah, which means insight, prudence, intelligence, or human comprehension. What we have here is the Lord saying, when we are going about our daily lives, we are not to lean to our own understanding, intelligence, or human comprehension. We are to consult God in everything. We should learn to use the wisdom of my high school basketball coach. Do not think that we know what the best course of action is for our lives. Always rely on God. He is much wiser and more intelligent than we could ever become or imagine.

We need to listen to Isaiah 55:8–9: "For my thoughts are not your thoughts, neither are your ways my ways, saith the Lord. For as the heavens are higher than the earth, so are my ways, higher than your ways, and my thoughts than your thoughts." Our spiritual roof that protects our souls must be anchored by putting our trust totally in the Lord.

PHASE 7

The Crowning Moment of Perfection and Completion

Now unto him that is able to do exceeding, abundantly above all that we ask or think according to the power that worketh in us.

—Ephesians 3:20

There are times in our Christian walk that we must stop and reflect on who God is to us and what is the purpose of our existence. With that in mind, the following events will show you that God had a master plan for my life. And at the time, I had no idea what the plan was. When I worked for the Union Pacific Railroad, I operated a machine called the locomotive car mover. It was my job to bring all the locomotives into the shop and put them in position for repairs. In doing so, I met a diesel mechanic named Edward

D. Lairry. At this time, I did not know that he was a pastor. We had a good working friendship at the railroad. Often after positioning locomotive cars for repair, I would stop and strike up a conversation with him. However, during those times, he never mentioned that he was a pastor of a church. I believe it was God's way of keeping him humble.

This next series of events in my life is what I called an act of God's divine providence or the sovereignty of God's will. He is always working behind the scenes to put his will in motion. One of our coworkers asked me if I had ever attended Ed Lairry's church. I was surprised to hear he was a pastor, but I was also inclined to go hear this humble guy preach. I got the location of the church, and my family and I attended the service the very next Sunday.

I can tell you, there was a big difference between Ed Lairry, the mechanic, and Edward Lairry the pastor. I was amazed at how this humble and gentle guy at work became this powerful man on fire for the Lord in the pulpit on Sunday mornings. After the sermon, he came down and greeted my family and me. He told me how glad he was to see us at church. At that time, I was not attending church at all.

From that day forward, our conversation changed on the job. I began to ask him more serious questions about the Bible and the Christian faith. This would become a crowning moment for me because eventually, along with my wife and children, we united with the church. It would be through Pastor Lairry's teaching and preaching of the

Gospel of Jesus Christ that my foundation would be laid. To top this crowning moment off, months later, my family and I were baptized into the Christian belief under the leadership of the late Pastor Edward D. Lairry.

As a young believer I was naïve in my faith assuming like most newbies, that once I united with the body of Christ, my life would become so much easier. I did not realize at the time that I had become a target of the enemy (perception can be an eye opener). What made matters worse was shortly after my family and I united with the church, I started to see behavior from church members that did not quite resemble Christianity. There were some people within the church that were still living by the standards of the world and then showed up for church on Sunday morning with their holy attire on.

The atmosphere in the church had become so turbulent. Eventually, the church experienced a split, and Pastor Lairry resigned as the pastor of New Hope. I could not understand how this could happen; I thought all Christians could come together through prayer and work things out. A few weeks after the split, Pastor Lairry invited several associate ministers and a few others to his home. I was among those that was a part of this meeting. He shared with us that God told him to organize a new church named Greater New Hope. I was in a spiritual pandemic of a different sort. I had to decide what would be best for my family and me. *I was trying to keep a level head of faith in the midst of a pandemic.*

But as things progressed, I was appointed as a deacon under the leadership of Pastor Lairry at the newly organized Greater New Hope Baptist Church. This situation allowed me to see the almighty power of God at work. The church quickly grew spiritually and physically. Later as I reflected on this, my first thought when the split occurred was devastation. But I got to see firsthand how God can turn a situation that appeared to look hopeless around and make it work for his glorification. This experience had a profound effect on my faith in God. Romans 8:28 reminds us, "And we know that all things work together for good to them that love God, to them who are the called according to his purpose."

These life-changing events prepared me for the next crowning moment that God had laid out for my life. In ancient Roman time, they divided the twenty-four-hour day this way: The first twelve hours were considered the morning watches (6:00 a.m. to 6:00 p.m.). The night watch was divided into four watches: 6:00 p.m. to 9:00 p.m. was the first watch. The second was 9:00 p.m. to midnight. The third was midnight until 3:00 a.m. And the fourth watch of the night was 3:00 a.m. to 6:00 a.m. This last watch was considered the darkest and stillest hours of the night.

In the Bible, Jesus performed mighty miracles during the fourth watch of the night. The most astounding was when Jesus saw his disciples either with his bodily eyes from the mountain he was on or he perceived in his Spirit what distress his disciples were in, and he came to their rescue.

As the account is told in Mark 6:48–51:

> And he saw them toiling in rowing; for the wind was contrary unto them: and about the fourth watch of the night, he cometh unto them, walking upon the sea, and would have passed them. But when they saw him walking upon the sea, they suppose it had been a spirit, and cried out: For they all saw him, and were troubled. [*Jewish tradition had a myth that if you saw a spirit on the water, it was that of a fisherman who had died while fishing on the lake. So I can see why the disciples would be afraid assuming that Jesus was a ghost.*] And immediately he talked with them, and saith unto them, Be of good cheer: it is I; be not afraid. And he went up unto them into the ship; and the wind ceased: and they were sore amazed in themselves beyond measure and wondered.

Jesus was there doing the fourth watch to calm the storm for his disciples. In the midst of our storms, Jesus is still here for us, even in the fourth watch of the night when we are usually asleep. We can rest assured he is here to see us through this pandemic.

Another example was in the Old Testament: It was the fourth watch of the morning that God performed a miracle for Moses and the Israelites during their escape from Egyptian captivity. Exodus 14:24 says, "And it came to pass, that in the morning watch the Lord looked unto the host of Egyptians through the pillar of fire and of the clouds and troubled the host of the Egyptians."

This miracle during the fourth watch was when God parted the Red Sea and allowed Moses and the Israelites to walk across on dry land. Shortly thereafter, the sea was closed again, and the Egyptians and all of the pharaoh's horses and horsemen were drowned in the Red Sea. God never sleeps nor slumber. He can always provide protection for his people. *"Remember, nothing happens on earth unless it has heaven's permission."*

This brings me to the night God called me to preach his Word. It was the fourth watch at 3:00 a.m. I was awakened out of a deep sleep; my spirit was overshadowed with the presence of the Lord; I experienced a surge of power that I had never felt before. This power arrested my spirit, even my sense of touch was no longer mine. It was the Lord's. I tried to awaken my wife, who is usually a light sleeper, but I could not awaken her. The Lord immediately put in my spirit; this miraculous experience was for me alone.

I was no longer in control of my own body. I felt like a stranger on the outside, looking in. The Lord had taken over and overshadowed me at that moment. I got out of the bed and began to walk toward my study. It felt as though I had so much power that I could have walked through a wall. I sat there, and I responded, "What would you have me to do, Lord?

And the voice of the Lord spoke to me and said, *How is your house built?*

I replied, "Whatever you would have me to do, Lord," because I was now sensitive to his voice.

God became my voice, and he spoke these words through me, *Therefore whosoever heareth these sayings of mine, and doeth them, I will liken unto him as a wise man, which built his house upon a rock: And the rain descended, and the floods came, and the winds blew, and beat upon that house and it fell not: for it was founded upon a rock.*

I later discovered this is recorded in his Holy Word in Matthew 7:24–25.

And again, he said, *How is your house built?*

I asked the Lord, "Are you calling me to preach your Word?"

He replied again, *How is your house built?*

I then said to the Lord, "I will preach your Word, and I accept my calling."

As I sat in my study, I said, "Matthew 7:27"

He spoke to me and said, *Matthew 7:24.*

I opened my Bible to Matthew 7:24, and I was astonished to find the same scriptures that the Lord had just spoken through me. This is amazing because I had never read this passage of scripture before. In obedience to the

Lord, the first sermon I preached was entitled "How Is Your House Built?"

I had just experienced an epiphany moment with God. That same morning when my wife awakened, I shared this awesome moment with her.

And she replied, "Why didn't you wake me up?"

I told her, "I tried to awaken you, but the Lord had placed you in a deep sleep. He also told me this experience was only for me."

When I reflect on that night, I think of God's first human creation, Adam. He was placed in a deep sleep, and God took one of his ribs and created "womb-man" or "woman" because she came from the womb of the man. I thank God for my wife, my helpmeet, my friend, my partner, and the rib that came from me. I am so blessed to say, from that day forward, my wife have supported me in the ministry.

Our marriage reminds me of the story of Cinderella. She left her golden slipper in the prince's chariot. He went about trying to find out whose foot would fit the golden slipper. Wanting the opportunity to be married to the prince, women lined up for miles to get the chance to see if they could fit the golden slipper. But only Cinderella's foot would fit the slipper. The moral of this story is, if the one you choose does not fit with the plan God has for your life, do not force it. Wait on God for your mate, and you will not have to force the slipper to fit. My wife, Cheryl

Ann Bennett, became my Cinderella story, and I am forever grateful to God.

"Remember, nothing happens on earth unless it has heaven's permission."

My mind thinks back on how this idea of writing this book came about. One morning, I was awakened by a phone call from one of my members. I counseled him and his wife and performed their marriage ceremony several years earlier. He informed me that he and his wife were going through some rough waters that had caused some serious turbulence in their marriage, and his wife was contemplating divorce. We can say that they were in the midst of a "personal pandemic."

His faith was shaken, and he sounded hopeless. We spent hours on the phone. I shared the wisdom of God's Word and prayed with him. He sounded a lot better when we finally finished our conversation. Later in the week, I got another phone call from this same member. I could tell in his voice that there was something seriously wrong, and he simply wanted me to listen. His voice was distraught, saddened, and grief-stricken. He sounded confused and was seeking comfort of some kind to help keep a level head of faith. He informed me that his son had been murdered the night before. I was so saddened and shocked. I quickly called upon the Lord to give me the words to console him and help provide strength within his inner spirit.

As I talked to him and consoled him, I realized he had three different pandemics going on in his life at the same time: COVID-19, his wife contemplating divorce, and now his son who had been murdered. His whole world was in complete chaos. What came to my mind at this time is the scriptures God had given me earlier that eventually became the foundation for a seven-week Bible study entitled "Keeping a Level Head of Faith."

As I continued consoling and talking to him, I looked out over the horizon. The sky was full of brightness, and I saw one of the most beautiful white clouds.

While standing there in my garage, the voice of the Lord spoke to me and said, *I want you to write a book.*

I was still having a conversation with this member, trying to console him, and the Lord was speaking to me saying that he wanted me to write a book in the midst of all of this conversation.

I asked the Lord in my inner spirit, *What would you have me to call this book?*

He replied, *Keeping a Level Head of Faith in the Midst of a Pandemic.*

As our conversations continued over the next few weeks, it became apparent God had used him in the midst of his personal pandemic, as an instrument or tool to inspire me to write this book. This was something I had never done or thought about doing. However, I am sensitive to God's voice, and I know that his will must be done. This gave me the confidence that this book is the commission of God. *Remember, nothing happens on earth unless it has heaven's permission.*

We have now arrived at this great anticipated moment: the seventh foundational scripture during our seven-week study. Anyone that knows me knows I am a numbers person. The number seven means completion. On the seventh week of our Bible study, I woke up that Wednesday morning, fired up like I had never been before. I could not wait until 6:00 p.m. to come for our Bible study; this is when the members would begin to check in for our conference call for a Bible study.

In Paul's letter to the church at Ephesus, the primary purpose was to strengthen their faith and spiritual foundation. He would do so by revealing the fullness of God's eternal purpose of redemption for the Church and for each individual member of its body. From the first three chapters of this epistle, Paul has put emphasis on three major points, beginning with Ephesians 1:3, "Blessed be the God and Father of our Lord Jesus Christ, who hath blessed us with all spiritual blessings in heavenly places in Christ;" Ephesians 2:20, "And are built upon the foundation of the apostles and prophets, Jesus Christ himself being the chief cornerstone;" and lastly, Ephesians 3:20, "Now unto him that is able to do exceeding, abundantly above all that we ask or think according to the power that worketh in us."

This is what we have learned from these three important scriptures: We have been blessed already in heavenly places, he is our foundation, which makes him the chief cornerstone, and no building can remain standing without the chief cornerstone. Finally comes Christ's crowning moment. He has no boundaries; his power is matchless and has no limitations—*keeping a level head of faith in the midst of a pandemic.*

It Is Time to Breathe Again

If our spiritual souls do not get the life-saving oxygen of God's Holy Word, we can suffer and die a spiritual death. Only his Word can open our spiritual nasal passages that strengthens our minds, bodies, and souls. Only through his strength can we raise our level of faith. Ephesians 3:16 says, "That he would grant you, according to the riches of his glory to be strengthened with might by his Spirit in the inner man."

For example, have you ever applied for grant money from the government? It is generally money that does not need to be paid back. But the catch is, you must make sure that you keep accurate records so that you can give an account for everything that you have done with it. God has given us grant money according to his riches and glory to strengthen our inner man by his Spirit. Christ paid our sin debt in full on the cross of Calvary. One day, we will have to give a full account of what we did with the grant money, not to the government but unto God. For that crowning moment, the Lord has said, "For it is written, As I live, saith the Lord, every knee shall bow to me and every tongue shall confess to God" (Romans 14:11).

In our seventh and final foundational scripture, Ephesians 3:20, Paul has broken this scripture into three major stanzas.

First, he says, "Now on to him that is able to do exceeding, abundantly." This teaches us that because of God's goodness and mercy, he desires and deserves our adoration and aspiration. He is the source of our strength and the breath of our life.

Romans 16:25 tells us, "Now to him that is of power to stablish you according to my gospel, and the preaching of Christ, according to the revelation of the mystery, which was kept secret since the world began." That is considered God's accommodations. Knowing all that God has provided for us, we should love and adore him always. Next, he says, "Above all that we ask or think." Our minds are limited. We are only able to see as far as our faith will allow us. The apostle Paul recorded in 1 Corinthians 2:9, "But as it is written, eye have not seen, nor ear heard, neither have entered into the heart of a man, the things which God has prepared for them that love him."

With God, you can see, through faith, beyond your human ability. God promises to do great things for those who wait for him. Believers must look to him and persevere in hope, confidence, and patience.

In the Old Testament passage of scripture, Isaiah 64:4 assures us this way: "For since the beginning of the world men have not heard, nor perceived by the ear, neither that hath the eye seen, O God, besides thee, what He hath prepared for him that waiteth for him." There had been moments in all our lives where our human ability could only carry us so far, and God had to supernaturally intervene. His intervention provided the hope and confidence to continue to do his will. This assures us that he will never leave nor forsaken us.

And in his last stanza, Paul says, "According to the power that worketh in us." God will only do that which is in us. You must develop your belief through trusting him. Your benefits will be limited to your level of belief. The term *power that worketh in us* is the resident power of the Holy Spirit. At the time of our confession, every true believer receives the indwelling of the Holy Spirit. The extended power comes with the effusion of the Holy Spirit and causes our body, soul, and spirit to merge. The Holy Spirit from God should become president and not just resident in our lives. The next step is water baptism; this is a demonstration of our conversion for others to see.

God is not daunted by time nor limited by space: "Now unto him that is able to do exceeding, abundantly above all that we ask or think according to the power that worketh in us." Notice the superlatives that Paul uses here: *exceeding, abundantly,* and *above*. When using grammatic superlatives, they are designed to enhance and express the highest or an extremely high degree of quality of an adjective or adverb.

Let us break this superlative down this way: *Exceeding*: the Greek word is *Huper*`, which means for the benefit of, for the sake of, or over more than beyond. God can carry us far beyond our limited imaginations. *Abundantly*: the Greek word is *Periss`os*, which means over its prefixed boundary, more exceeding, superabundantly, or to overflow over and above. God can provide an overflow based on our belief. *Above*: the Greek word is *Huper`*, which is the same word as *exceeding* with a slight difference. It means supersede, limitless, no range or restrictions, above the minimum but higher, and the maximum.

This tells us, during this pandemic, when we begin to panic, our faith can drop to a dangerous level. This can cause fear and anxiety, which can cause us to sin against God. He implies "I AM HE" who is much more than enough to handle all your worries. To help us when we are experiencing a lack of faith, Paul recorded in 2 Corinthians 4:17–18, "For our light affliction, which is but for a moment, worketh for us a far more exceeding and eternal weight of glory. While we look not at the things which are seen, but at the things which are not seen: for the things which are seen are temporal: but the things which are not seen are eternal."

We should not focus our attention on the current state of our world, but our faith will allow us to see the things that are not seen.

God is saying, *Although you cannot see me, I am still working behind the scenes for your life.*

All the things that we experience in this life are only temporary, but those things that are not seen are eternal.

God is saying three words, *I got this.*

"Nothing happens on earth unless it has heaven's permission."

In every spiritual house, there must be a king, and that king is Jesus Christ. We must crown him with adoration of love. We must seek him with a heart of aspiration because we cannot live without him. He has earned this adoration and seeking of aspiration because of the price he paid with his precious blood on Calvary for our accommodations in heaven.

Ephesians 3:20 tells us, "Now unto him that is able to do exceeding, abundantly above all that we ask or think according to the power that worketh in us." This promise to us is conditional and dependent upon the degree of faith that causes the Holy Spirit's presence, power, and grace operating in our lives.

Keep in mind, because of the predestination of God, meaning his foreknowledge of things to come, he is the only one who knows how our end will come. None of us can play the role of God, so we must trust him. Isaiah 40:8 says, "The grass withereth, the flower fadeth: but the word of our God shall stand forever." Trust God during your personal, physical, spiritual, and even in the midst of a worldwide pandemic. Amen.

EPILOGUE

What has happened to our country? We are a people that have fallen prey to our own devises. We are a nation that has turned away from God and has made man, money, and monuments our gods. How do we dig ourselves out of this deep hole that we have fallen into? We must repent of our sinful behaviors and pray that God will pardon us for all our evil doings. We must remove bigotry, hatred, and ischemic racism from our hearts. "We must not be defined by the color of our skin but by the content of our character." These are the spoken words of the late Dr. Martin Luther King Jr.

God gave us the best he had—his only begotten Son in the presence of Christ Jesus who shed his precious blood for the remission of our sin. Whatever denomination or religious affiliation you may be associated with or even if you are a nonbeliever, there is still a fabric or mode in which we all have been woven from. As we look beyond the starry heavens of our solar system, we can all come to this conclusion that we all came from the same Creator.

We must come to a common ground that somewhere over the rainbow, there is still a God who rules and has control of the heavens and the earth. This dreadful disease or plague that has come over our land and taken the lives of hundreds of thousands of people has not shown any sign of prejudice or discrimination. If COVID-19 can be on one accord with its agenda, why can't we, as a people, come together to be on one accord?

Keeping a Level Head of Faith in the Midst of a Pandemic: Phase 1

You must ask yourselves, How can we keep a level head of faith in the midst of a pandemic? We must build a new foundation, a foundation made by God, a foundation of stone, a tried stone that has stood the test of time, and a precious cornerstone that is a sure foundation, as recorded several times in God's Holy Word (1 Peter 2:4–6, Romans 9:33, 1 Corinthians 3:11, and Ephesians 2:20).

Keeping a Level Head of Faith in the Midst of a Pandemic: Phase 2

"The Lord is my rock and my fortress, my deliverer; my God, my strength, in whom will I trust; my buckler, and the horn of my salvation, and my high tower" (Psalm 18:2). We must develop a personal relationship with God so that our enemies cannot penetrate our spiritual house (Hebrews 2:13 and Psalm 62:2).

Keeping a Level Head of Faith in the Midst of a Pandemic: Phase 3

"And the Lord, he it is that doth go before thee; he will be with thee, he will not fail thee, neither forsake thee: fear not, neither be dismayed" (Deuteronomy 31:8). The Lord is the only one that can protect our going and our coming, so we are not to live in fear (Joshua 1:5–9 and Ezekiel 13:21).

Keeping a Level Head of Faith in the Midst of a Pandemic: Phase 4

"For God hath not given us the spirit of fear; but of power and of love, and of a sound mind." God has given us the trinity of faith: the spirit of power, the spirit of love, and the spirit of a sound mind. So do not let Delila (fear) in your spiritual house (2 Timothy 1:7, Romans 8:15, 1 John 4:18, and Acts 1:8).

Keeping a Level Head of Faith in the Midst of the Pandemic: Phase 5

"The Lord he is my light and my salvation; whom shall I fear? the Lord is the strength of my life; of whom shall I be afraid?" Living in the light allows us to see and feel our eternal freedom while still exposing our enemies. (Psalm 27:1, Isaiah 60: 19, Exodus 15:2, and Psalm 62:2).

Keeping a Level Head of Faith in the Midst of a Pandemic: Phase 6

"Trust in the LORD with all thine heart; and lean not unto thine own understanding." Trust in the Lord is a promise. He is our protector and our provider, so allow him to be the pilot whereby we can be his passengers. (Proverbs 3:5, Psalm 37: 3–5, and Jeremiah 9: 23).

Keeping a Level Head of Faith in the Midst of a Pandemic: Phase 7

"Now unto him that is able to do exceeding, abundantly above all that we ask or think according to the power that worketh in us." God's power is limitless. He has no boundaries. He is an able God. He is not handicapped. He is not hindered. So be sure to allow the Holy Spirit room to work within your spiritual house (Ephesians 3:20). All adoration and aspiration belong to him because of all the accommodations he has given us. Who would not serve a God like that? (Romans 16:25, 1 Corinthians 2:9, and Colossians 1:29).

God's Word is powerful when fully believed and spoken. God being the Architect and Creator of all things that exist called into action his Word. When problems arise in our lives, we must search God's Word for the solution to rescue us from the perils of our dilemmas. When one tries to trust in their own ability to sustain themselves, they will always stumble and fall. We must always turn to the self-existent One who is Christ Jesus our Lord.

Belief in the Word of God is vitally imperative while coexisting in an ecosystem that has no control over the environment. Man was created in the image of God but was given freedom to execute his own decisions in life.

Being independent in the world is the American dream. But when the world begins spinning out of control, what does one do?

We turn to our faith in God. As our measure of faith matures, we can reap all the benefits of God's Holy Word.

Benediction: We should never allow politics to influence our decisions but rather the Word of God. Colossians 1: 16–17 (KJV) says, *"For by him were all things created, that are in heaven, and that are in earth, visible and invisible, whether they be thrones, or dominions, or principalities, or powers: all things were created by him, and for him: And he is before all things, and by him all things consist."*

God used man to create things in the world for his divine purpose, even the very vaccines we take and the masks we wear for our additional protection.

"Now unto Him that is able to keep you from falling, and to present you faultless before the presence of His glory with exceeding Joy. To the only wise God, our Savior, be glory and majesty, dominion, and power, both now and ever. Amen" (Jude 1:24–25).

ABOUT THE AUTHOR

Image of the author: Rev. Isiah Bennett Jr.
Book: *Keeping a Level Head of Faith in the Midst of a Pandemic*

Rev. Isiah Bennett Jr. is a skilled preacher and teacher anointed by God. He has been preaching and teaching the Word of God for over twenty years. He started as a deacon at Greater New Hope Baptist Church, North Little Rock, Arkansas. He was a dedicated deacon who stood by and supported the vision of his pastor. In this position, he learned all aspects concerning the administration and day-to-day operations of the church. This experience was invaluable when the Lord called him to pastor. He pastored the flock at Shady Grove Baptist Church in Tucker, Arkansas, for two years. Through the leadership of the Holy Spirit, the Church experienced spiritual and physical growth during his tenure. In September 2007, the Lord moved him to Greater New Hope in Little Rock, Arkansas. Rev. Bennett believes the Bible is the infallible Word of God and should be followed completely. He is a member of the Greater Little Rock Baptist Pastoral and Ministers Conference. He has studies in Old Testament and New Testament survey, basic theology, and fundamentals of faith, as well Christological preaching, which is seeing Christ throughout the whole Bible. He is self-educated through the divine power and inspiration of the Holy Spirit. He is articulate in the hermeneutics, which is the methodological breakdown of the Holy Scriptures.

He is married to Cheryl Bennett; they have five adult children and thirteen grandchildren. All their children that live here locally are actively involved in the ministry. As Greater New Hope Baptist Church follows the vision that the Lord has given Pastor Bennett, the church will continue to grow spiritually and physically. The Lord has blessed Pastor Bennett with a special gift for reaching young adults with the Word of God.

COMMITTED TO EXCELLENCE.